Contents

Words in **bold** are in the glossary.

What's so special about spiders?

Some people are afraid of spiders. But very few spiders are dangerous. Most are helpful. Spiders eat insects that may spread diseases and eat crops.

Spiders are not **insects**. Insects have three main body parts. Spiders have two. Insects have six legs. Spiders have eight. Spiders belong to a group of animals called **arachnids**.

There are about 46,700 known **species** of spiders. They live all over the world except in the coldest places.

DID YOU KNOW?

Spiders feed mostly on insects. They eat about 880 million tonnes of insects each year.

Smithsonian

LITTLE EXPLORER

SPLENDID SPIDERS

by Melissa Higgins

Raintree is an imprint of Capstone Global Library Limited, a company incorporated in England and Wales having its registered office at 264 Banbury Road, Oxford, OX2 7DY – Registered company number: 6695582

www.raintree.co.uk
myorders@raintree.co.uk

Edited by Abby Huff
Designed by Kyle Grenz
Original illustrations © Capstone Global Library Limited 2021
Picture research by Tracy Cummins
Production by Katy LaVigne
Originated by Capstone Global Library Ltd
Printed and bound in India

978 1 4747 9463 3 (hardback)
978 1 4747 9476 3 (paperback)

British Library Cataloguing in Publication Data
A full catalogue record for this book is available from the British Library.

Acknowledgements
We would like to thank the following for permission to reproduce photographs: iStockphoto: OGphoto, 7; Minden Pictures: Pete Oxford, 20, Reg Morrison, 29, Stephen Dalton, 17 (bottom); Nature Picture Library: Stephen Dalton, 19; Shutterstock: asawinimages, 17 (top), BEJITA, 13, Brberrys, 24, Chalermchai Chamnanyon, 10 (top), Colin Dewar, 9, davemhuntphotography, 21, Heather Broccard-Bell, 10 (middle), Jamikorn Sooktaramorn, 6 (top), Jay Ondreicka, 25, John Dorton, cover, Joseph Potter, 6 (middle), Marco Maggesi, 23, Ondrej Michalek, 15, Peter Yeeles, 11, pratan ounpitipong, 1, Richard Constantinoff, 5 (top), Sarah2, 2, shaftinaction, 27, Vinicius R. Souza, 10 (bottom), Vova Shevchuk, 5 (bottom), Zeren, 6 (bottom)

Our very special thanks to Gary Hevel, Public Information Officer (Emeritus), Entomology Department, at the Smithsonian National Museum of Natural History. Capstone would also like to thank Kealy Gordon, Product Development Manager, and the following at Smithsonian Enterprises: Ellen Nanney, Licensing Manager; Brigid Ferraro, Vice President, Education and Consumer Products; and Carol LeBlanc, Senior Vice President, Education and Consumer Products.

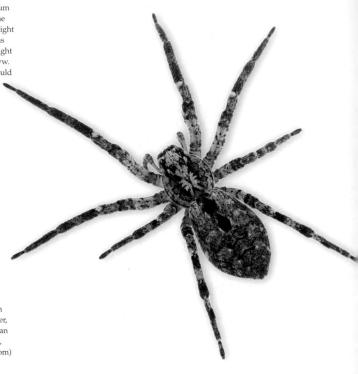

A spider's body

Spiders have two main body parts. The front part is the head. The back part is the **abdomen**. Spiders have eight legs. Most have eight eyes. They do not have ears. Instead, fine hairs on their legs sense sound.

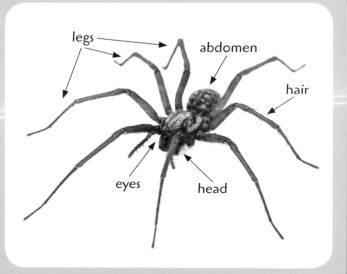

legs
abdomen
hair
eyes
head

Amazing Webs

Spiders are famous for the webs they build. Webs are made of a fine thread called silk. Spiders make silk inside their bodies. They shoot it out from a body part called a **spinneret**. Spiders build webs to catch food.

Lots of webs

There are three main types of webs. Orb webs are round and sticky. Insects stick to them. Tangled webs are a mess of silk. The jumbled threads trap insects. Funnel webs are flat on top with a small tube to the side. Spiders run out of the tube and catch **prey** that walk across the top.

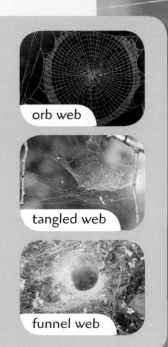

orb web

tangled web

funnel web

All spiders make silk. Only some use it to make webs. Other spiders use silk to make homes. Females wrap silk around their eggs to keep them safe.

spinneret

DID YOU KNOW?

Spider silk is the strongest fibre in nature. It is even stronger than steel.

Orb weavers

Number of species: 3,100
Found: worldwide except in the coldest climates
Body length: 0.3 to 3 centimetres (0.12 to 1.18 inches)

Have you ever run into a sticky web? It probably belonged to an orb weaver. This spider uses different types of silk to make its round web. The outer threads of silk are strong to hold the web in place. The inner threads are sticky to snag prey. Most orb weavers build their webs at night. It can take them a few hours.

DID YOU KNOW?

Some orb weavers use their webs more than once. Others build a new web each night.

Wolf spiders

Number of species: 2,300
Found: worldwide except in the coldest climates
Body length: 0.64 to 3.5 cm (0.25 to 1.38 inches)

Wolf spiders don't build webs. They hunt. The wolf spider chases insects on the ground. It grabs them with its strong legs. Wolf spiders eat crickets, ants and grasshoppers.

A spider's life

A female spider lays many eggs. She wraps them in a silk sac to keep them safe. The eggs hatch. Baby spiders look like tiny adults. Young spiders are covered with a stiff outer shell. They have to **shed** the shell in order to grow. Most spiders live for 1–2 years.

egg sacs

young

adult

A female wolf spider carries her eggs in a silk **sac**. The baby spiders hatch and climb onto her back. She carries them around. The young spiders leave when they can live on their own. That can take up to two weeks.

DID YOU KNOW?

Like many spiders, wolf spiders are most active at night.

Jumping spiders

Number of species: more than 5,800
Found: worldwide except in the coldest climates
Body length: 0.3 to 1.9 cm (0.12 to 0.75 inches)

The jumping spider can leap up to 50 times its own body length. Its legs act like springs. Blood rushes into the spider's legs and they snap out straight. It happens so fast that the spider shoots into the air.

Jumping spiders are hunters. They see prey and leap at it. Their sharp eyes can zoom in on small things.

DID YOU KNOW?

There are more jumping spiders than any other type of spider in the world. They come in many shapes, sizes and colours.

Crab spiders

Number of species: 2,166
Found: worldwide except in the coldest climates
Body length: 1.3 to 2.5 cm (0.5 to 1 inches)

Can you see how this spider got its name? Its flat body and big legs make it look like a crab. It walks sideways like a crab too.

Crab spiders don't build webs. Most don't chase prey. They wait for prey to come close. Then they grab it! Crab spiders are good at hiding. Some slowly change colour to match the leaves, grass or flowers where they live.

DID YOU KNOW?

Spiders have many **predators**. Frogs and toads eat them. Birds and rodents do too. Even spiders eat other spiders.

Pirate spiders

Number of species: more than 160
Found: worldwide except Antarctica
Body length: about 0.4 cm (0.15 inches)

Making a web to catch food takes a lot of work. Pirate spiders don't bother. They eat a web's owner instead. A pirate spider first finds the web of a smaller spider. It plucks one of the web's threads. When the web's owner scurries over to check out the movement, the pirate spider grabs it and kills it with strong **venom**.

DID YOU KNOW?

The venom of pirate spiders is more harmful to other spiders than it is to insects.

Venom!

Most spiders use venom. Venom is a poison. The spider's body makes it. The spider shoots venom through its hollow fangs. Venom stuns prey and turns its insides to mush. Spiders suck up the mush. Most spider venom is not strong enough to hurt people.

Water spiders

Number of species: 1
Found: Europe and Asia
Body length: 0.76 to 1.52 cm (0.3 to 0.6 inches)

This is the only spider that spends its whole life underwater. Most water spiders live in ponds and slow streams. How do they do it? The water spider swims close to the surface. Fine hairs on its body trap air bubbles. The spider dives back down and fills its web with the bubbles. The web puffs out like a balloon. The spider lives inside the web and breathes the stored air.

DID YOU KNOW?

Baby water spiders often live in empty snail shells before they build their first web.

A water spider fills its underwater web with air bubbles.

Tarantulas

Number of species: about 900
Found: warm climates
Body length: 2.5 to 10.2 cm (1 to 4 inches)

These spiders are big. Their bodies are hairy. But there is little to fear. Tarantulas don't often bite people. Their venom is weaker than the venom in most bee stings. But watch out for tarantula hair! Some end in sharp points. Tarantulas can flick the hairs to drive enemies away.

Spidery giant

The goliath birdeater is a tarantula, and it's one of the biggest spiders in the world. Its legs span up to 28 cm (11 inches). That is bigger than an average man's hand! They live in South America.

Tarantulas are hunters. They eat insects and larger prey such as lizards, snakes and frogs. Most tarantulas dig **burrows** and live underground.

– DID YOU KNOW? –
Female tarantulas can live for up to 25 years.

Tarantulas are called monkey spiders in South Africa.

Trapdoor spiders

Number of species: 128
Found: worldwide except in the coldest climates
Body length: about 3 cm (1.2 inches)

The trapdoor spider likes to hide. It digs a burrow and lines the walls with silk. The spider finishes its home with a door made of silk and soil. It blends in with the ground. The spider lays silk threads around the door. An insect walks by and touches a thread. The trapdoor spider notices the movement. It dashes out in a flash and grabs its prey!

DID YOU KNOW?

The world's oldest-known spider was a trapdoor spider. It was 43 years old when it died. It lived in Australia.

Widow spiders

Number of species: 31
Found: worldwide except in the coldest climates
Body length: 0.64 to 2.5 cm (0.25 to 1 inches)

Watch out for female widow spiders. Their venom is very strong. Their bites can make it hard for a person to breathe. Luckily, most widow spiders only bite when a person scares them.

You can spot a female black widow spider by a red mark on her belly. The mark is shaped like an hourglass.

Widow spiders make tangled webs. These are also called cobwebs.

— **DID YOU KNOW?** —

Most people recover from widow spider bites. Deaths are very rare.

Funnel weavers

Number of species: 1,150
Found: worldwide except in the coldest climates
Body length: 0.4 to 2 cm (0.15 to 0.8 inches)

This spider's web is flat on top and narrow at the bottom. It looks like a funnel. The funnel weaver builds its web in the grass or on a bush. It waits in the narrow part of its web. An insect walks over the non-sticky top. Extra threads of silk slow it down. The web shakes, and the spider notices. It quickly runs out and grabs its prey.

DID YOU KNOW?

Some funnel weavers lay silk lines above their webs. Flying insects hit the lines and fall onto the webs.

27

Net-casting spiders

Number of species: 57
Found: tropical and sub-tropical climates
Body length: 2 to 2.5 cm (0.8 to 1 inches)

Watch out, insects! You won't see this spider until it's too late. The net-casting spider hangs upside down. It holds a small web between its long front legs. The web acts like a net. The spider stretches it wide and then snaps it over passing prey.

Net-casting spiders have huge eyes. Those big eyes help them see at night while they hunt. They have the biggest eyes of any spider.

Taking aim

The net-casting spider uses its poo to help its aim. It drops a dot of its white poo beneath where it hangs. The dot acts like a target in the dark. The spider throws its net when an insect crosses over the dot.

DID YOU KNOW?

This spider's creepy-looking face has earned it another name: the **ogre**-faced spider.

Glossary

abdomen end part of a spider's body

arachnid group of animals that includes spiders, scorpions, mites and ticks

burrow hole in the ground that an animal makes and uses as a home

insect small animal with a hard outer shell, six legs, three body sections and two antennae

ogre person or thing that is scary and mean

predator animal that hunts other animals for food

prey animal hunted by another animal for food

sac pouch made of silk that holds spiders' eggs

shed when the shell or fur of an animal falls off and is replaced by a new shell or fur

species group of living things that can reproduce with one another

spinneret part of a spider's body that squirts out silk

venom poisonous liquid made by some animals

Comprehension questions

1. In what ways are spiders good for the environment?

2. Many spiders do most of their hunting and web building at night. Why do you think that is? Why might the day be a bad time to be active?

3. Describe how the trapdoor spider catches its prey.

Find out more

Books

Arachnids (Animal Kingdom), Pamela Dell (Raintree, 2018)

Assassin Bug vs Ogre-faced Spider: When Cunning Hunters Collide (Minibeast Wars), Alicia Z. Klepeis (Raintree, 2017)

Insects and Spiders: Explore Nature with Fun Facts and Activities (Nature Explorers), DK (DK Children, 2019)

Websites

www.dkfindout.com/uk/animals-and-nature/arachnids/spiders
Find out about all different types of spiders.

www.bbc.co.uk/newsround/29413435
Watch this video for five facts about spiders.

Index